Encyclopædia Britannica

Fascinating Facts

History

PUBLICATIONS INTERNATIONAL, LTD.

Encyclopædia Britannica, Inc.
310 South Michigan Ave.
Chicago, IL 60604

Printed and bound in USA.

8 7 6 5 4 3 2

ISBN: 1-56173-325-3

SERIES PICTURE CREDITS:

Academy of Natural Sciences; Allsport U.S.A.;
Animals Animals; Art Resources; Donald Baird;
John Batchelor; Blackhill Institute; Ken Carpen-
ter; Bruce Coleman, Inc.; Culver Pictures; Kent
& Donna Dannen; FPG International; Brian
Franczak; Howard Frank Archives/Personality
Photos, Inc.; Tony Freeman/PhotoEdit; Douglas
Henderson/Museum of the Rockies/Petrified
Forest Museum Association; Carl Hirsch; Blair
C. Howard; International Stock Photography;
Eleanor M. Kish/Canadian Museum of Nature,
Ottawa, Canada; Charles Knight/Field Museum
of Natural History; Vladimir Krb/Tyrell Mu-
seum; Manfred L. Kreiner; T. F. Marsh; NASA;
Gregory Paul; Paul Perry/Uniphoto; Christian
Rausch/The Image Works; Peter Von Sholly;
SIU/Custom Medical Stock Photo; Daniel
Varner; Bob Walters; Peter Zallinger/Random
House, Inc.

A Wonder of the World

The pyramids were built to remind the citizens left behind just how rich and powerful the Pharaoh had been. Since the ancient Egyptians believed in life after death, they wanted people to be as comfortable as possible in the afterlife. As a result, a person's favorite belongings, as well as much-needed items like clothing and food, were buried with him or her. Egypt's kings and queens obviously wanted to live well in the afterlife, since they put everything they might possibly want, including gold and jewels, ships, and servants, in their tombs. To hold all of this—and to keep all of these things safe from robbers—they built large, safe tombs.

Many workers were needed to construct a pyramid.

The Pharoahs of Egypt

The Pharaohs were the kings and rulers of ancient Egypt, governing more than 5,000 years ago. These rulers had complete, total power and were even treated as gods and goddesses by their people. Despite many wars and conquests, the Pharaohs ruled Egypt until the coming of the Roman Empire, 3,000 years later.

The Curse of the Tomb

Not long after King Tut's tomb was found, the leader of the expedition who discovered it, Lord Carnarvon, died from the effects of a mosquito bite. Other members of the group also met mysterious fates. As a result, some people began to believe that the ancient Egyptians had placed a curse on the tomb. According to this curse, anyone who disturbed King Tutankhamen's tomb would soon meet a violent and terrible fate. No one today, of course, takes the curse very seriously.

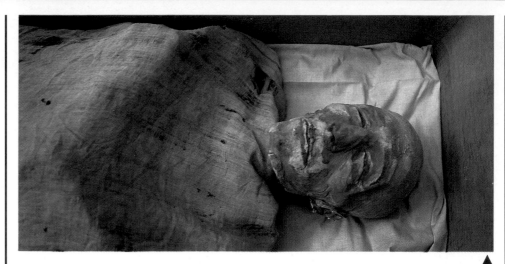

Preserving Mummies

Because they believed that people could live after death, the Egyptians preserved the bodies of those who had died. They first soaked these mummies in herbs and chemicals, wrapping the bodies in bandages and placing them inside a coffin. The coffins were often painted to show the face and body of the person whose body was inside. The Egyptians also made mummies of people's favorite pets, so they could accompany their masters to the afterlife. These pet mummies were then set out close to the main coffin.

The Amazing Tomb of King Tut

King Tutankhamen (or "King Tut" as he is called by modern people) ruled Egypt 2,400 years ago. He died young, at about the age of 18, and was buried with all of the riches and goods he would need in his afterlife. His tomb was discovered in 1922 by an English archaeologist, Howard Carter. The things that were found—as well as the young King's preserved body—created a sensation. Many of these things can now be seen in the world's best museums.

The Persian Empire

The Persian Empire was one of the largest and most powerful kingdoms of the ancient world. Founded in 553 B.C. by the emperor Cyrus, it eventually stretched from Asia Minor to India and relied on good roads and a complex military and political system to maintain its power. The Persians produced some of the greatest pottery, porcelain, and literature of that period in history, and they were known for their fair treatment of the nations they conquered. Until the time of Alexander the Great, Persia was the greatest empire the world had ever seen.

A Very Mighty Empire

Alexander was the King of Macedonia, a small, warlike country to the north of Greece. He became one of the greatest conquerors in the history of the world. Educated in Athens by the great philosopher Aristotle, Alexander became ruler of Macedonia and Athens in 336 B.C. He then set out to conquer the world. He led his armies across to Asia and, in 333 B.C., defeated the Persians, who had the largest empire in the world at that time. He then proceeded south and east, conquering almost all of the known world of the time. By the time he died at the age of 33, his empire spread from Greece to Egypt and as far as India.

The Fall of an Empire

Wherever he went, Alexander spread the Greek culture and way of life. However, his empire was not able to survive without him. After his death, his generals divided the empire among themselves. Soon, it was nothing more than a group of small, weak nations fighting against one another.

The death of Alexander the Great

Reading the *Iliad*

The *Iliad* is the story of the war between one group of city-states and the great city of Troy, which was located in what is now Turkey. The book is a long poem that describes the battles and events, as well as the heroes of that war.

Odysseus feigned madness by plowing the seashore.

Adventures of Odysseus

The *Odyssey* tells of the adventures of one of the Trojan War's great heroes, Odysseus, as he made his way home from Troy.

Government of the People

Unlike other ancient nations, Athens was not ruled by a king or emperor. Instead, it had a special governing council. All male citizens were also part of an assembly that made Athens' laws. This meant that everyone—nobles, merchants, and even simple farmers—had a voice in their government.

These people are looking at the objects that Schliemann found at Troy.

The Height of Greek Civilization

In the 400s B.C., the city-state of Athens reached new heights of strength and civilization. Art, plays, and philosophy were flourishing. Athens also had a great deal of military power. Unfortunately, Athens grew too confident and was led into a war with another Greek city-state, Sparta. It was defeated and never quite recovered its glory.

A Great Discovery

In 1873, a German scientist named Schliemann discovered the ruins of Troy—a city whose citizens fought a ten-year war with ancient Greece. Over the years, dozens of scientists have examined the ruins. Finally, an American expedition concluded that the walled city was in fact the Troy of the *Iliad.*

Hippocrates was the father of modern medicine.

Ancient Greek Learning

In ancient Greece, learning and knowledge were highly valued, especially in the city-state of Athens. In fact, Greek philosophers and scientists made contributions to knowledge that we are still using today. Democritus, for example, came up with the idea of atoms 2,400 years before the atomic bomb. Pythagoras helped create the geometry that we still study in school today. Herodotus wrote the world's first history books, trying to find out the truth of what happened in the past. Hippocrates started modern medicine, showing people how to cure injuries and illnesses scientifically, instead of with prayers and magic.

7

Rome's Most Famous Ruler

Julius Caesar was one of ancient Rome's greatest soldiers and leaders. After an early career in politics, Caesar set out to become a military leader. In less than ten years, he had conquered what is now France, Belgium, and parts of The Netherlands, Germany, and Switzerland. He even led troops across the English Channel to invade Britain. Later, he turned his attention eastward and added territories in the Middle East to Rome's growing empire. In 45 B.C., he was made permanent head of Rome's government and began to be treated as a god by the people. This made other politicians jealous and led to his murder by a group led by one of Caesar's closest friends, Marcus Brutus.

Mark Antony and Cleopatra

The Queen of the Nile

For thousands of years, Cleopatra has been a symbol of beauty, power, and romance. She became a queen of Egypt at the age of 17, but it was her love affairs with Julius Caesar and, later, Mark Antony, that made her so famous. Cleopatra and Antony joined together to try to take over the entire Roman Empire. They were unsuccessful, however, and they both committed suicide.

A Roman Extravaganza

The Colosseum was a giant, round theater built around 70 A.D. It was large enough to seat 50,000 viewers, and it was the scene of thousands of battles between gladiators, fights between men and animals, and other spectacles. At times, it was even flooded with water so that navies of gladiators could battle one another. Lightning, earthquakes, and vandalism have left it a ruin, but it still stands in Rome today.

Ruling the Roman Empire

During the early days, Rome was a Republic, ruled by a Senate and consuls who were elected to office. As Rome grew weaker, however, the Republic became weaker. Professional soldiers often helped bring leaders to power by force of arms. Senators and business people took power in order to make profits for themselves. By the time of Julius Caesar, political battles in Rome often led to civil war. Finally, Julius Caesar's adopted son, Octavian, took power. He ruled Rome for 45 years and brought peace. By the end of his life, the Republic was over, and Rome had become an Empire ruled by an Emperor.

A Terrible Emperor

The worst Roman emperor was probably Caligula, who came to power at the age of 25. He began his rule quite well, but illnesses seemed to bring about a mental breakdown after a few months. After that, he behaved in a dangerous and violent manner. He murdered his relatives, made his favorite horse a high public official, and fought in the arena as a gladiator. In one of his more outrageous acts, he made a bridge of ships across the Bay of Naples. He filled the ships with houses and trees, and announced that he was now able to cross the sea on dry land. To celebrate his accomplishment, he threw a giant party on the ships and had hundreds of his guests thrown into the sea and murdered. Four years later, he was murdered by an officer of his imperial guards.

Respected Roman Emperors

The emperors Trajan and Hadrian brought good government back to Rome after years of corruption. Marcus Aurelius was another excellent emperor, a wise man who was a successful politician and general as well as a philosopher.

Marcus Aurelius

9

Vicious Vikings ▲

Between the years 700 and 1000 A.D., warriors from Norway, Sweden, and Denmark called Vikings attacked people all through northern Europe. Sometimes, they simply attacked and stole whatever they wanted; other times, they took over land and settled themselves as farmers and landowners. These Vikings were among the most fierce and cruel fighters the world had ever seen. Viking attacks usually meant that homes were burned, churches and other buildings were robbed, and dozens of people were killed or taken away as slaves. As you might expect, people were terrified whenever they heard that Vikings were near.

Viking Settlements ▲

Unlike other conquerors, the Vikings never built up a single organized empire. They did, however, sail all the way to Greece and Turkey, using the rivers and seas of Eastern Europe. They traded with Greek and Arab merchants there and brought many goods back home to Scandinavia. They also set up settlements in Iceland and Greenland. Many experts believe that they sailed as far as North America, building settlements in Labrador and Newfoundland.

Leif Eriksson.

Vikings Everyone Knows

Erik the Red, who founded the Viking settlement in Greenland, is one of the best-known Vikings, as is his son, Leif Eriksson. Leif is supposed to have been the leader of the Viking expedition that reached North America.

Fierce Genghis Khan

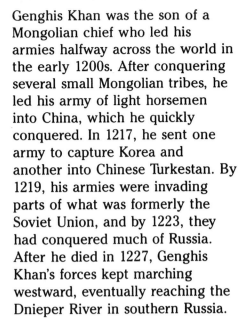

Genghis Khan was the son of a Mongolian chief who led his armies halfway across the world in the early 1200s. After conquering several small Mongolian tribes, he led his army of light horsemen into China, which he quickly conquered. In 1217, he sent one army to capture Korea and another into Chinese Turkestan. By 1219, his armies were invading parts of what was formerly the Soviet Union, and by 1223, they had conquered much of Russia. After he died in 1227, Genghis Khan's forces kept marching westward, eventually reaching the Dnieper River in southern Russia.

Renowned Mongol Soldiers

Unlike other armies of the time, Genghis Khan's soldiers wore lightweight armor and rode small, fast horses. Most of his soldiers were born horsemen, able to ride for days at a time without rest. (In fact, stories say that they often did not even stop to cook food; they merely drank a little horse's blood and rode on.) They were also fierce warriors, totally destroying the cities and lands they conquered. When the city of Herat, Afghanistan, rebelled against the Mongols, Genghis Khan's soldiers burned and looted for a week, killing over 1.5 million people. Their violent actions made them the most feared fighters in the history of the world.

Popular Kublai Khan

Kublai Khan, the grandson of Genghis Khan, became the ruler of the Mongol empire in 1259. Not content with the kingdom that had been passed down to him, Kublai Khan sent armies to the south, finishing the conquest of China. He was a superb ruler, but he was also intelligent and tolerant. He was very popular with his Chinese subjects, as well as among his own Mongol people. Kublai Khan admired Chinese culture so much that he gradually adapted himself and his own people to it.

Knights fought bravely in the Crusades.

An Honorable Knighthood

By the year 1000, the Church began to put forward a new kind of knighthood. Laws were passed that protected people from the actions of knights. The idea of knights as protectors of the less fortunate was spread. Most importantly, the knights themselves were convinced to join in a great Crusade to free the Holy Land of Palestine from Muslim rule. All of these factors worked to change Europe's knights from rough, violent bullies to more well-behaved and noble individuals.

On Becoming a Knight

Once a young man had become a knight, he was supposed to live a model life. According to his vows, his primary job was to help make the world a better place to live. This meant fighting against his master's enemies, following the rules and regulations of his religion, and helping those in need. Since knights were still supposed to fight, much of their time was spent making themselves stronger and better fighters.

A young man is knighted.

Life in the Middle Ages

The Middle Ages began when the Roman Empire fell apart, and went on for almost a thousand years. This was a rough, violent time in Europe. Almost 90 percent of the people were peasants—farm laborers who worked on the lands of rich nobles. These peasants were not free at all, bound to their lords and the land from birth. Food and clothing were scarce, and life was always a battle for survival. The nobles, as you might expect, lived better, but they certainly didn't have an easy life. They had clothing and food, but little else. Their homes were cold, they had little entertainment, and they were almost constantly at war with foreign invaders or greedy neighbors who wanted to take over their land. All of this made life so hard that few people ever lived a very long life.

Games, Dances, and Song ▲

Knights and nobles kept themselves busy with games, dances, and, especially, singing. By the 1200s, most knights were well trained in singing, playing the lute, and writing their own songs. (If a knight was not especially talented in music, he could hire a professional singer to provide the voice and music.) Other forms of entertainment included festivals, banquets, and contests that tested knights' skill with the lance and sword.

Fighting the Holy Wars

The Crusades were a series of religious wars that took place between 1095 and 1270. Their goal was to keep the Turks and other Muslims from invading Europe and to return the holy city of Jerusalem to Christian control. Over the years, there were many Crusades, and battles were fought everywhere from Egypt to Jerusalem to Constantinople (the present-day city of Istanbul). In the end, the Muslim armies proved too strong and they eventually gained complete control of the Middle East by the 1500s.

Knights defended their castle fiercely.

▼

King Richard the Lion-hearted

King Richard I of England was nicknamed "Lion Heart" because he was a brave and successful soldier. Whether he was as well loved by his people as legends say is not known, especially since he spent most of his life away from England—at one war or another. What we do know is that he won many battles in France, Italy, and Palestine and that he was killed attacking a castle in France.

Armor protected knights in battle.

The Queen of the Golden Age

When Queen Elizabeth I came to power, England had been through several years of unrest. She quickly brought order and set out to make England the greatest power in the world. She also loved music, poetry, and dance. Under her rule, England enjoyed a time of great cultural triumph. Even in her own time she was applauded as the queen of England's "golden age."

The Famous King Henry VIII

Stories describe King Henry VIII as a fat man who had many wives. In truth, Henry was a handsome young man when he came to the throne in 1509 at age 18. Moreover, he was well educated and was a talented poet and musician. He was also a skilled athlete who often won contests that were held at the royal court. His marriage problems were caused by his desire to leave England a male heir who would become king after him. Because his first wife had no sons, he divorced her to marry someone else. This put him in conflict with the Pope, starting years of problems. Unfortunately, Henry did not always find peaceful solutions to problems, sending many men and women to their deaths. Surprisingly, despite all these troubles, he remained quite popular with the people—and the nobles—for most of his life.

Men Who Should Not Have Been King ▲

King George III was one of the worst kings of England, since his policies helped bring about the American Revolution. Another poor ruler was Richard III, who is supposed to have killed his own young nephews in order to make his way to the throne. Going further back in history is another very bad king, King William II, the son of William the Conqueror. William II came to the throne at the age of 31, already famous for his wicked life. His years on the throne were spent making plots against his brother Robert, the Duke of Normandy, and setting up harsh new taxes in England. His rule ended when he was found killed by an arrow at the age of 44. No one confessed to the murder, but most people believed that it was ordered by William's brother, who later became King Henry I.

The Long Reign of Queen Victoria ▼

Queen Victoria had the longest reign of any British ruler. Coming to the throne in 1837 at the age of 18, she ruled for 64 years until her death in 1901. She was among Britain's most popular monarchs, despite the fact that people seemed annoyed at her way of hiding from the public. The 50th and 60th anniversaries of her coronation were treated as major national holidays, with celebrations going on all through the vast British Empire.

The Sun Never Sets on the British Empire

By the middle of the 1800s, when Queen Victoria was named Empress of India, the British Empire stretched all around the globe. In fact, one of the old sayings was that "the sun never sets on the British Empire"—meaning that the sun was always shining at some point in the world where the British flag flew.

Britain's Famous Leader

Winston Churchill was a symbol of Great Britain's refusal to surrender to its enemies during World War II. He broadcast speeches on the radio, made public appearances, and convinced the United States to provide as much aid as possible. His words urged people all over the world to fight the Nazis (whose name he insisted on mispronouncing, as a kind of insult) and their allies. In one of his most famous speeches he told the world that "we shall defend our island whatever the cost may be, we shall fight on the beaches...we shall fight in the fields and in the streets, we shall fight in the hills; we shall never surrender." After the war, the British people wanted a change and voted his Tory party out of power in 1945.

The Three Napoleons

Besides the famous Napoleon Bonaparte, there were two other French emperors named Napoleon. Napoleon II (1811-1832) was the only son of Napoleon I (Bonaparte) and his second wife, the empress Marie-Louise. At birth, he was named King of Rome. When his father abdicated the throne, Napoleon II was named his successor. He never ruled France, however, since the French people chose to be ruled by Louis XVIII instead. Napoleon III (1801-1873) was the nephew of Bonaparte. After two unsuccessful attempts to overthrow the monarchy, he fled to England. After the Revolution of 1848, he returned to France and was first elected to the National Assembly and later to the presidency. He crowned himself emperor of France as Napoleon III in 1852.

Coronation of Napoleon and Josephine ▲

In December 1804, Napoleon crowned himself Emperor of France. He also crowned his wife, Josephine, Empress of France.

Napoleon's Famous Pose ▼

Pictures of Napoleon often show him with his right hand stretched across his stomach and placed in his coat or shirt. In fact, this picture is so familiar that people have been making jokes about it for over a hundred years. The reason for this pose is that portrait painters thought it looked dignified and saved them from the job of drawing someone's hand (which can be quite a difficult task). If you look at the portraits in an art museum, you will probably see dozens of other people holding their hands in exactly the same way.

The Height of the French Empire ▲ ▬

At one time, Napoleon's conquests stretched from the English Channel in the west all the way to Moscow, Russia. Italy, Spain, and even Denmark and Norway were tied to him. This gave him one of the largest empires seen in Europe since the days of the ancient Romans.

Liberty, Equality, Fraternity

The French Revolution was fought because the peasants and workers decided to throw off the rule of the royal family and the whole system that seemed to keep them poor, overtaxed, and attacked. Hundreds of France's nobles, including the king and queen, were killed, and a new government—a Republic—began.

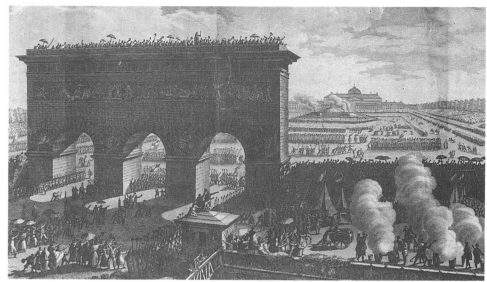

Let Them Eat Cake

According to stories told in the late 1700s, Marie Antoinette, the Queen of France, was a spoiled woman who loved luxury. When she was told that the people of France had no bread to eat, she replied, "Let them eat cake," a message that seemed to say that there was no problem of hunger and that everyone lived as well as she did. Marie Antoinette, who was particularly disliked, was beheaded during the French Revolution.

A Famous French Statesman

Many people consider Charles de Gaulle the greatest hero of modern France. When Germany invaded France at the beginning of World War II, de Gaulle refused to admit defeat. France itself surrendered, but de Gaulle gathered thousands of Frenchmen in England. Calling themselves the "free French," they continued to fight. When the Allies invaded Europe and marched to free France from the Nazi armies, de Gaulle's free French army marched with them. After the war, de Gaulle helped organize a new French government. During the 1950s, the French people called on de Gaulle again. He came out of retirement to lead France one last time.

A Civilized King

Frederick the Great was King of Prussia from 1740 to 1786. (At this time, there was no Germany, only a group of different states of which Prussia was the largest and strongest.) A wise and strong ruler, he was known as a skilled military leader and for his fondness for literature and the arts. In fact, when he was young he tried to run away from the royal court so that he could pursue his scholarly interests. Throughout his life, Frederick worked hard to develop and modernize his country. He encouraged agriculture and education. He also did much for primary education and the study of science. He called himself "the first servant of the State" and made the Prussian government extremely efficient.

The Iron Chancellor

In Germany, the chief political leader is called "chancellor," and the "Iron Chancellor" was Otto von Bismarck, the man who led Germany for almost 30 years. He was a firm leader who often overruled the German emperor (or "Kaiser"). His policies made Germany into a strong, wealthy country. In 1890, however, the young Kaiser Wilhelm II decided that he wanted to rule without the advice of his strong Chancellor and threw Bismarck out of office.

Heil Hitler!

The word *Nazi* is an abbreviation for the German words meaning "National Socialist German Workers' Party." Adolf Hitler became president of the group in 1921. Hitler took advantage of the hard times Germany had after World War I to convince the German people that only he could restore German power and wealth. Part of his plan, however, were racist policies that declared that all other nationalities, races, and ethnic groups were inferior to Germans. He also believed that Germans would ultimately rule the world. The actions of the Nazis led to World War II and the death of millions of people.

The Age of the Aztecs ▼

The Aztecs, arriving in Mexico during the 1200s, were one of the most important people in North America before the arrival of Europeans. Although they started out as a poor, weak tribe, they soon began conquering the land of other groups in the area, as well as making new farmland by creating man-made islands in the giant lakes of central Mexico. By 1325, they were building their great capital city near what is now Mexico City. They remained powerful rulers until the Spanish defeated them in the 1500s.

The Aztec Way of Life ▲

The Aztecs were a highly advanced people. They built marvelous cities, had a successful system for draining lakes and making new farmland, and were excellent astronomers—predicting eclipses and seasons. They were also a fierce people with a very strong army, which allowed them to use captives as human sacrifices to their many gods.

Reading Mayan Glyphs ▲

For many years, scientists believed that the Maya were peaceful farmers, quite different from their violent Aztec neighbors to the north. Recently, however, scientists have learned to read Mayan "glyphs," picture-writings that they left on buildings and stone tablets. These writings give us a different picture of Mayan life. They describe a warlike people who practiced a violent religion that included both human and animal sacrifice.

The Mayan Years ▲

The Maya were an important group living in America before the coming of Europeans. Their empire reached from southern Mexico to Guatemala and Belize. The Maya reached their height between 300 A.D. and 900 A.D.

The city of Cuzco today
▲

Inca and the City of the Sun ▲

The "City of the Sun" was Cuzco, the capital of the Inca Empire in South America. Around the year 800 A.D., the Inca people began building a wonderful civilization. At its peak, it stretched from Bolivia to parts of Argentina and Chile. They were ruled by a king called the Inca, who was believed to be a god descended from the sun. This ruler, who had total power of life and death over his people, lived in the sacred "City of the Sun."

A Place for Everyone ▲

The Inca were a highly organized people. Every group of ten families had a leader who reported to a captain. The captain was responsible for five leaders—a total of 50 families. The Inca himself was the ultimate ruler. Everything belonged to the state in the Inca system. Everyone worked, and a certain amount of everything the people produced went to the Inca himself and to his government.

The End of the Inca

In the 1500s, the Spanish leader, Francisco Pizarro, had the Inca rulers killed so that Spain would be in complete control of the Incan people, land, and gold.

The Ruins of Machu Picchu ▼

In 1911, Hiram Bingham of Yale University discovered an Incan city. High in the Andes mountains, between two high, rough mountain peaks, he came upon the city of Machu Picchu where a temple, a fortress, and terraced gardens were found.

Vikings on American Soil

For many years, American children were taught that Christopher Columbus discovered America in 1492. Evidence, however, points to settlements on this continent long before that time. According to ruins and records, it seems that Vikings landed in North America around the year 1000. According to the "Tale of the Greenlanders," which tells many stories of the Vikings' voyages, Leif Eriksson learned of a place called "Vinland" (Wine-land) and set out to find it. The tales say that he landed in that area, setting up a fort for Viking settlers. Later trips were made by Leif's brother and another Viking explorer, Thorfinn Karlsefni. For years, people looked for proof that Vinland existed. Recently, ruins were found in Newfoundland and Labrador, Canada.

History Repeats Itself

The first *Mayflower* carried the Pilgrims from Southampton, England, to Massachusetts in 66 days. In 1957, a copy of the ship was built and sailed from England to the United States in honor of that first voyage. The *Mayflower II* proved faster than its ancestor, making the journey in just 53 days. Since then, it has been used as a floating museum and tourist attraction.

The Landing of the *Mayflower*

The Pilgrims were one of several groups in England who wanted to break away from the country's official church, the Church of England. They made plans to set up a new home for themselves in North America—on the Hudson River, in what is now New York State. However, when their ship, the *Mayflower*, finally reached the New World, it landed at Cape Cod, in Massachusetts. Since the captain of the ship was unwilling to risk taking the ship any farther along the coast, the Pilgrims set up their colony at Plymouth, Massachusetts.

The Mayflower braved treacherous seas to reach the New World.

Organized Minutemen

By 1774, feelings against Great Britain were so strong that the militia of Worcester County, Massachusetts, decided that part of their militia should always be ready to fight at a moment's notice. The men soon got the name "Minutemen." After the Minutemen fought against British soldiers at the Battles of Lexington and Concord, other colonies began setting up Minutemen units of their own.

The Green Mountain Boys

The Green Mountain Boys were a militia set up in the early 1770s in Vermont. Originally, they got together to keep New York from claiming land in Vermont. When the Revolution broke out, they actually took part in the first real military action of the war. Led by Ethan Allen and Benedict Arnold, 100 Green Mountain Boys, along with 100 other volunteers, captured Fort Ticonderoga, on May 10, 1775.

The Father of Our Country

George Washington was a rare individual, able to be both a skilled general and a brilliant politician. As commander in chief of the American forces during the Revolution, he managed to win a victory against England, the most powerful army in the world. Much of the credit was in Washington's ability to get people to work and fight together despite differences of opinion. Later, when Washington became the first president of the United States, he faced an even more difficult job. The Constitution described what kind of government the country would have, but it was up to Washington to actually set up that government.

The Site of Washington, D.C. ◀

The people writing the U.S. Constitution decided that the capital of the nation should not be in either the North or the South. George Washington himself chose the site for the new city, Washington, D.C., selecting the French architect Pierre Charles L'Enfant to plan it.

A Famous American Fighter ▼

Andrew Jackson was famous as a fighter long before the War of 1812. As a boy during the Revolution, he was struck with a saber by a British officer when young Jackson refused to clean the officer's boots. Later, he became a general in the Tennessee militia. In 1814, he put down a rising of Creek Indians and became famous as an Indian fighter. It was this reputation that led to his command at the Battle of New Orleans. In 1818, he led a group of soldiers into Florida, chasing a group of Indian raiders. Even though this action caused problems since Florida was a Spanish territory, the arguments over the situation eventually led to Florida's becoming part of the United States.

Attacking the Nation's Capital

During the War of 1812, U.S. forces invaded Canada several times. To get even, the British sent a force of 4,000 soldiers to take the American capital, Washington, D.C. In August 1814, they arrived by ship and captured the city easily, burning the Capitol, the president's house, and other important buildings. The attack came as a complete surprise, and it was a terrible blow to the young nation's pride.

The Defeat of Tecumseh ▼

Tecumseh was a Shawnee leader who tried to save Indian lands from being completely taken over by white settlers. In the early 1800s, he organized the Ohio, Michigan, and other tribes to act against white settlements. In 1811, warriors led by his brother were defeated by General William Henry Harrison, and Tecumseh's power was broken. He was finally killed during the War of 1812.

Thomas Jefferson

America's 50th Anniversary ▲

July 4, 1826, was the 50th anniversary of the Declaration of Independence, and celebrations went on throughout the United States. On that day, however, two former presidents died—Thomas Jefferson, the author of the Declaration of Independence and the nation's third president, and John Adams, one of the leaders of the Revolution and the country's second president.

▲ *John Quincy Adams*

John Adams

The Celebrated Adams Family

The Adams Family of Massachusetts was one of the most remarkable groups in the history of the United States. It included two presidents, John Adams and John Quincy Adams; Charles Francis Adams, a member of Congress and a diplomat; Charles Francis Adams, Jr., a president of the Union Pacific Railroad; Henry Adams, a writer and historian; Brooks Adams, a historian and radical thinker; and Charles Francis Adams III, Secretary of the Navy during the 1920s.

The March of the Nez Perce

Chief Joseph was the leader of the Nez Perce Indians who tried to lead his people all the way from their home in the Northwest to Canada. For three months, an army of more than 5,000 soldiers chased the 500 Nez Perce over Oregon, Washington, Idaho, and Montana. When Chief Joseph finally surrendered, his people had marched over 1,000 miles.

Putting Up a Good Fight ▲

A leader of the Chiricahua Apaches, Geronimo was famous for his raids on white settlers. Although he was caught many times, he also managed to escape on numerous occasions. In all, 5,000 soldiers and 500 Indians chased after Geronimo and his band of 35 men, eight boys, and many women. He was finally captured and sent first to Florida and then to Alabama. Although he tried to escape several times, he finally settled into a life of peace and quiet.

Custer's Last Stand ▲

When gold was discovered in South Dakota, hundreds of white settlers entered the area. This led to Indian attacks, and a large army was sent to protect the settlers against the Indians. Lieutenant Colonel George Armstrong Custer, along with 600 men, was sent out to scout for Indians. One group of Custer's force attacked a group of Indians near the Little Bighorn River in Montana. They found, to their horror, that instead of a few hundred warriors, there was a force of almost 2,500. They retreated, as did another group of soldiers. Custer, along with 226 soldiers under his command, attacked. In the fighting that followed, Custer and all of his men were killed. This battle was called Custer's Last Stand.

Honest Abe

From his youth, Abraham Lincoln was known for his personal honesty. According to some sources, the nickname "Honest Abe" was given to him in childhood; others say that Lincoln was given this name for his integrity as a young lawyer. In any event, Lincoln was known as "Honest Abe" by the time he first served in the United States Congress in 1847.

All Men Are Created Equal

In 1863, Lincoln issued the Emancipation Proclamation, which freed slaves in all of the states fighting against the Union. It did not officially end slavery, since some of the states remaining in the Union still had laws permitting slavery. It did, however, give the states that had joined the Confederacy a strong message that the days of slavery were over.

The Death of a President

Lincoln was shot on the night of April 14, 1865, just a few months after the final surrender of the Confederate armies. The man who shot the president while he was at the theater was an actor named John Wilkes Booth. Born in Maryland, Booth had devout Southern sympathies and saw Lincoln as a man who would destroy the defeated states. He had originally planned to kidnap Lincoln and hold him for the ransom of Confederate soldiers held in prison camps in the North. Since this scheme failed, Booth decided to assassinate the president. Eight people were found guilty on June 30, 1865, of conspiring with Booth to kill Lincoln.

Our Fallen Heroes

Lincoln was the first United States president to be murdered in office—unfortunately he was not the last. On July 2, 1882, President James Garfield was on his way through the train station in Washington D.C., when a stranger came up and fired two shots. The murderer, a man named Charles Guiteau, shot the president because he had not been given a job as U.S. Consul in Paris. Nineteen years later, another president was murdered. On September 5, 1901, President William McKinley gave an important speech at the Pan-American Exposition in Buffalo, New York. The next day he attended the fair again, taking a tour of the Temple of Music. While McKinley was shaking hands with people in the crowd, a man named Leon Czolgosz reached out his hand and shot the president. Eight days later, McKinley died. The most recent president to be murdered was John F. Kennedy, who was shot on November 22, 1963, while driving through the streets of Dallas, Texas. The man who was arrested for the murder, Lee Harvey Oswald, was shot a few days later.

The New Frontier

While he was running for president, John F. Kennedy used the words "New Frontier" as he urged Americans to think of the future in the same way as earlier Americans had—and to accept the challenge to change the world for the better.

A Square Deal

The words "square deal" were made famous by Theodore Roosevelt, the 20th president of the United States, when he declared that he would make sure that there would be a "square deal" for everyone, rich and poor alike.

The New Deal

When Franklin D. Roosevelt was elected president, the United States was suffering from hard times. To confront the problems, Roosevelt declared that there would be a "new deal"—new policies that would make things better for everyone. For many years, Roosevelt worked to make the "new deal" a reality.

Exploring for France

In 1534, the French explorer Jacques Cartier sailed up the St. Lawrence River, exploring the area. He returned there later and set up a fort on a piece of high ground that he named *Mont Real,* or "mount royal." The place has been called Montreal ever since.

Canada's Two Languages

The area of what is now Canada was originally explored and settled by the French, and for many years the area belonged to France. At the end of a series of wars between France and Britain, the territory was given to Great Britain. As one of the terms of the treaty, Britain promised that the Canadians (or French-Canadians, as they are sometimes called) would be allowed to keep their own religion, laws, and language. As a result, there are many French-speaking areas in Canada today.

The Royal Canadian Mounties

You probably have seen pictures of Canada's famous "Mounties," their national police, in their bright red coats. Although the Mounties do not wear these uniforms for their everyday work, they do wear them on dressy occasions.

Friendly Neighbors

Although the United States and Canada have had good relations for the past one hundred years, this was not always the case. During the American Revolution, American forces invaded Canada several times. During the War of 1812, part of Canada became a battleground between American and British soldiers. In the 1800s, there were several disagreements over borders in Maine and Oregon. At one point, the United States seemed willing to go to war over its borders in the Northwest. Since the 1870s, however, any disagreements that have come up have been handled without threat of war or violence.

Pancho Villa

Emiliano Zapata

Heroes of Mexican Liberty

Pancho Villa and Emiliano Zapata were important leaders of the Mexican Revolution. Beginning in 1909, Villa helped overthrow several Mexican dictators, including the much-hated Porfirio Diaz. Zapata was a *mestizo*, a peasant who made his living training and raising horses. He organized other peasants into a powerful political party that fought for the liberty and rights of the Mexican people. Villa was killed in 1923. Zapata was murdered by political enemies in 1919. Both are considered heroes of Mexican liberty.

The Halls of Montezuma

The "halls of Montezuma," words made famous by the official song of the U.S. Marine Corps, were the domain of the Aztec Indians, near what is now Mexico City. Montezuma was the last king of the Aztecs, the people who ruled Mexico before the Spanish invaders arrived in the 1500s. Stories differ about what happened when the Spanish leader, Cortez, arrived in Mexico City. Some say that Montezuma was killed by his own people because they were angry that he did not fight against the Spanish. Others say that it was the Spanish themselves who killed the Aztec king. Either way, after Montezuma's death, the Spanish had little trouble in conquering the huge country once ruled by the Aztecs.

The Liberator of South America

Simon Bolivar, a Venezuelan born in 1783, was the great liberator of South America. Through his efforts and advice, Bolivia, Colombia, Ecuador, Panama, Peru, and Venezuela were all able to overthrow their Spanish masters and become independent countries. An idealist and unselfish man, Bolivar died penniless.

Setting South America Free

Simon Bolivar

Through the efforts of Simon Bolivar and General Jose de San Martin, South America was free of Spain by 1826. At the same time that Simon Bolivar was helping free the nations of northern South America, General Jose de San Martin was defeating the Spanish in Argentina, Chile, and Peru. While fighting against the Spanish in Argentina, San Martin realized that Argentina would never be free of Spain unless Peru and Chile were also free. So, he marched his Army of the Andes across the mountains and freed Chile from Spanish rule. He then led his men up the coast of Peru, where Bolivar helped him free that country.

The Many Faces of Brazil

Unlike most of the other countries in Latin America, Brazil was discovered and colonized by Portugal, not Spain. As a result, Portuguese, not Spanish, is the official language of the country. Many other languages are spoken by the Indian groups who still live there and the immigrants who came to Brazil from Italy, Germany, Spain, and even Poland and Japan.

Evita Peron

Hugely popular, Eva or "Evita" Peron was the wife of Juan Domingo Peron, who took power in Argentina in 1946. She organized labor unions, worked to get Argentine women the right to vote, and helped raise money to build schools and hospitals. She also forced the closing of newspapers and radio stations that opposed the Perons. She died in 1952, a few years before her husband's dictatorship was overthrown.

Dr. Livingstone, I Presume

In 1866, the Scottish explorer David Livingstone set out on his third expedition into the heart of Africa. Soon, however, all word from him stopped. The *New York Herald,* one of the leading newspapers in the United States, sent its best reporter, Henry Morton Stanley, to find out what had happened to Livingstone. After marching through the jungle for many months, Stanley finally found Livingstone on the shores of Lake Tanganyika. Livingstone was seriously ill and was grateful for the food and medicine Stanley brought, although he was not yet ready to return to civilization. Eighteen months later, Livingstone died. Stanley took up Livingstone's work, exploring the land and waterways of Central Africa for the next 15 years. His adventures made him one of the best-known and admired men in the world.

Henry Morton Stanley

David Livingstone

South African Freedom Fighter

The name of Nelson Mandela is linked to the cause of freedom in South Africa. The son of a South African tribal chief, he became a lawyer in the 1940s and began working against the South African government's policy of "apartheid"—the system that kept black and white South Africans completely separate from one another. Mandela's activities led to his trial for treason in 1961, which found him innocent and set him free. He was arrested again in 1962 and sent to prison for five years. While he was in jail, he was also charged with planning to use violence to overthrow the government of South Africa. In 1964, he was sentenced to life in prison, although he was released in 1990.

The Land Down Under

Although people had lived in Australia for thousands of years, Europeans first learned of the continent in the 1500s. Between 1516 and 1530, Portuguese sailors mapped part of the coast. Later, Spanish, Dutch, and English explorers also visited the area. Captain James Cook, the most famous of these adventurers, explored the area in the 1770s.

Gem of a Business ▲

Besides being a South African politician, Cecil Rhodes was the organizer of the famous De Beers diamond mining company. After many years of struggle, he managed to create the world's largest diamond company, gaining almost complete control of the diamond mining industry. Without him, there would have been far fewer diamonds mined in the world.

Fascinating Aborigines

When Europeans first arrived in Australia, there were almost 300,000 native people, or "Aborigines" as they were called. These people had come to Australia thousands of years before and lived by hunting, gathering food, and fishing. Conflicts between the new settlers and the Aborigines almost always ended up in the settlers' favor.

Australian Independence ■

Australia did not become an independent country until January 1, 1901. On that day the different provinces and areas were joined together into a single nation and were made a part of the British Commonwealth.

A
Aborigines, 31
Adams, Brooks, 24
Adams, Charles Francis, 24
Adams, Charles Francis III, 24
Adams, Charles Francis Jr., 24
Adams, Henry, 24
Adams, John, 24
Adams, John Quincy, 24
Afghanistan, 11
Africa, 30, 31
Alabama, 25
Alexander the Great (King), 5
Allen, Ethan, 22
Antony, Mark, 8
Apache Indians, 25
Apartheid, 31
Argentina, 20, 30
Aristotle, 5
Arnold, Benedict, 22
Asia, 5
Assassination, 8, 9, 15, 26, 27
Astronomy, 19
Athens, 5, 6, 7
Aurelius, Marcus (Emperor), 9
Australia, 31
Aztec Indians, 19, 29

B
Battle of New Orleans, 23
Belgium, 8
Belize, 19
Bingham, Hiram, 20
Bismarck, Otto von, 18
Bolivar, Simon, 29, 30
Bolivia, 20, 29
Bonaparte, Napoleon, 16
Booth, John Wilkes, 26
Brazil, 30
Britain, 8, 14, 15, 22, 28
Brutus, Marcus, 8

C
Caesar, Julius (Emperor), 8
Caligula (Emperor), 9
Canada, 21, 23, 25, 28
Carnarvon (Lord), 4
Carter, Howard, 4
Cartier, Jacques, 28
Chile, 20, 30
China, 11
Churchill, Winston, 15
"City of the Sun," 20
Civil War, 26
Cleopatra (Queen), 8
Colosseum, 8
Colombia, 29
Columbus, Christopher, 21
Constantinople, 13
Cook, James (Captain), 31
Cortez, Hernando, 29
Creek Indians, 23
Crusades, 12–13
Culture
  Chinese, 11
  Greek, 5
Curses, 4

Custer, George Armstrong
  (Lieutenant Colonel), 25
Cyrus (Emperor), 5
Czolgosz, Leon, 27

D
De Beers Company, 31
Declaration of Independence, 24
de Gaulle, Charles, 17
Democritus, 7
Denmark, 10, 16
Diamonds, 31
Diaz, Porfirio, 29
Divorce, 14

E
Ecuador, 29
Egypt, ancient, 3, 5, 13
Elizabeth I (Queen), 14
Emancipation Proclamation, 26
Emperors, 5, 8, 9, 16, 18
Empire
  Aztec, 19, 29
  British, 15, 31
  Greek, 5
  Inca, 20
  Mayan, 19
  Persian, 5
  Roman, 3, 8–9, 12
England, 8, 14, 15, 21, 22, 28
Entertainment, medieval, 13
Eriksson, Leif, 11, 21
Erik the Red, 11
"Evita," 30

F
Florida, 25
Fort Ticonderoga, 22
France, 8, 13, 16, 17, 28
Frederick the Great (King), 18
"Free French," 17

G
Genghis Khan, 11
Geometry, 7
George III (King), 15
Germany, 8, 17, 18, 30
Geronimo, 25
Glyphs, 19
Greece, ancient, 5, 7, 10
Greenland, 10, 11
Green Mountain Boys, 22
Guatemala, 19
Guiteau, Charles, 27

H
Hadrian (Emperor), 9
Harrison, William Henry, 24
Henry I (King), 15
Henry VIII (King), 14
Herodotus, 7
Hippocrates, 7
Hitler, Adolf, 18

I
Iceland, 10
Idaho, 25

Iliad (Homer), 6
Incas, 20
India, 5, 15
Indians
  Apaches, 25
  Aztec, 19, 29
  Creek, 23
  Incas, 20
  Mayans, 19
  Nez Perce, 25
  Shawnee, 24
Italy, 13, 16, 30

J
Jackson, Andrew, 23
Japan, 30
Jefferson, Thomas, 24
Jerusalem, 13
Joseph, Chief, 25
Josephine (Empress), 16

K
Karlsefni, Thorfinn, 21
Kennedy, John F., 27
Kings, 4, 5, 13–15, 16, 18, 29
Knights, 12–13
Korea, 11
Kublai Khan, 11

L
Labrador, 10, 21
L'Enfant, Pierre Charles, 23
Lexington and Concord,
  battles, 22
Lincoln, Abraham, 26
Livingstone, David, 30
Louis XVIII (King), 16

M
Macedonia, 5
Machu Picchu, 20
McKinley, William, 27
Maine, 28
Mandela, Nelson, 31
Marie Antoinette (Queen), 17
Marie-Louise (Empress), 16
Maryland, 26
Massachusetts, 21
Mathematics, 7
Mayans, 19
Mayflower, 21
Medicine, 7
Mexico, 19, 29
Military systems, 5, 7, 8, 19
Minutemen, 22
Mongolia, 11
Montana, 25
Montezuma (King), 29
Mummies, 4
Murder
  Caesar, Julius, 8
  Garfield, James, 27
  Kennedy, John F., 27
  Lincoln, Abraham, 26, 27
  McKinley, William, 27

Richard III, 15
William II, 15
Muslims, 12, 13

N
Napoleon Bonaparte (Emperor
  Napoleon I), 16
Napoleon II (Emperor), 16
Napoleon III (Emperor), 16
National Socialist German
  Worker's Party, 15, 17, 18
Nazis, 15, 17, 18
Netherlands, 8
"New Deal," 27
Newfoundland, 10, 21
"New Frontier," 27
New Orleans, battle, 23
New York, 21, 22
Nez Perce Indians, 25
Nobles, 12–13, 14, 17
Norway, 10, 16

O
Octavian (Emperor), 9
Odyssey (Homer), 6
Oregon, 25, 28
Oswald, Lee Harvey, 27

P
Palestine, 12, 13
Panama, 29
Pan-American Exposition, 27
Peasants, 12, 17, 29
Peron, Eva, 30
Peron, Juan Domingo, 30
Peru, 29, 30
Pet mummies, 4
Pharaohs, 3
Philosophy, 7
Pilgrims, 21
Pizarro, Francisco, 20
Plymouth Colony, 21
Poland, 30
Political systems, 5, 6, 8, 17
Portugal, 30
Presidents, 22, 24, 26, 27
Prussia, 18
Pyramids, 3
Pythagoras, 7

Q
Queens, 8, 14–15, 17

R
Racism, 18
Religion, 12, 19, 21, 28
Revolution
  American, 15, 22, 23, 24, 28
  French, 17
  Mexican, 29
Rhodes, Cecil, 31
Richard III (King), 15
Richard I (King), 13
Roosevelt, Franklin D., 27
Roosevelt, Theodore, 27
Royal Canadian Mounties, 28
Russia, 11, 16

S
Sacrifice, human, 19
San Martin, Jose de, 30
Schliemann, Heinrich, 7
Shawnee Indians, 24
Slavery, 26
South Dakota, 25
Soviet Union, 11, 16
Spain, 16, 30
Sparta, 7
"Square Deal," 27
Stanley, Henry Morton, 30
Suicide, 8
Sweden, 10
Switzerland, 8

T
Tecumseh, 24
Tombs, 3
Tories, 15
Trajan (Emperor), 9
Trojan War, 6
Troy, 6, 7
Turkey, 10
Tutankhamen (King), 4

U
Union Pacific Railroad, 24
United States, 15, 28
  Congress, 24, 26
  Constitution, 22, 23

V
Venezuela, 29
Vermont, 22
Victoria (Queen), 15
Vikings, 10–11, 21
Villa, Pancho, 29
Vinland, 21

W
Wars
  American Revolution, 22, 23, 28
  Civil, 26
  1812, 23, 24, 28
  Greek, 7
  Holy, 13
  Indian, 24, 25
  medieval, 12
  Mongolian, 11
  Persian, 5
  Roman, 8
  Trojan, 6
  Viking, 10
Washington, 25
Washington, D.C., 23
Washington, George, 22
Wilhelm II (Kaiser), 18
William II (King), 15
William the Conqueror, 15
World War I, 18
World War II, 15, 17, 18

Z
Zapata, Emiliano, 29